HOW
THE CROSS
CAME OUT
OF THE
CRUCIFIXION

By Carl Scovel
and Friends

How the Cross Came Out of the Crucifixion

Published by the Evangelical Missionary Society
in Massachusetts

Designed by Victoria Sax   Printed by BookBaby

ISBN: 9781735188621 (paperback), 9781735188638 (Ebook)

Library of Congress Control Number: 2024912386 (print), 2024912859 (Ebook)

Copyright © 2024

PREFACE

The cross stands at the center of Christian faith. Behind the cross stands the crucifixion. Behind the crucifixion stands a life, a life like yours and mine, but so much more. That life has power to transform lives including yours and mine. To know that power, however, we begin with the cross and crucifixion.

I grew up singing hymns about the cross such as "In the cross of Christ I glory." On the sign before our church in the Fenway you will read "Though the cross joy came into the world." Our retired priest calls the cross "the tree of life" and says "His death on the cross proves that the last word is not death but life."

These claims may baffle anyone who asks, "If the crucifixion wasn't a tragedy, what was it?" I found my answer to that question in the letters of the first missionary, St. Paul. I found it also in the lives of my heroes and heroines. I found it even for myself when recently diagnosed with a life-threatening cancer. Healing and empowerment can come out of suffering.

Since I think best through writing I began to write down my reflections. I sent them to fifteen friends who agreed to write their commentaries on my thoughts. Their insights are part this text.

Tom Wintle, a longstanding friend and colleague, convinced the trustees of the Evangelical Missionary Society to publish this text. Founded in 1807 in Lancaster, Massachusetts, the Society aims to "furnish the means of Christian Knowledge and moral improvement by the distribution of pious and religious tracts." I'm grateful to Tom and the trustees for their support and I hope that this small volume justifies their faith.

CONTENTS

INTRODUCING THE CROSS

The cross is the simplest symbol in human culture. When it consists of two lines of equal length set at right angles, the cross indicates the intersection of two roads. On maps it designates the four points of the compass. It represents the four points of the zodiac. In computations it tells us to add. It may be the simplest symbol of the human form.

Set that symbol on its side and it becomes X in the Western alphabet, a substitute for one's signature on a document, an instruction to multiply and a marker on ballot sheets. It is also the cross of St. Andrew in England.

The swastika is one form of a cross. Centuries before the National Socialists in Germany co-opted it, the swastika appeared in the ancient cultures of India, Africa, Europe and native Americans.

The letter T is a cross. Jesus died on a T-shaped cross. Place a small loop above the T and you have the symbol for the sun, which meant life in ancient Egypt.

The Roman cross is common in Christendom. It consists of two lines, the horizontal bisecting the vertical just above the midpoint. We see this cross on altars, steeples and gravestones, at wayside chapels and the scenes of roadside deaths. It is woven into the robes and stoles of priests and hangs from the necks of both the chic and the faithful. Churches and cathedrals are often designed in the form of this cross.

Crosses may be embellished with jewels, figures and scriptural scenes. The cross that once hung in the chapel of King's Chapel's parish house bore an inscription from Dante's Comedy, "E la sua voluntate e nostra pace." "In His will is our peace."

Christian crosses take many forms: the Lorraine, Orthodox, Maltese, Celtic, the splendid Jerusalem cross and others.

The cross in Christendom is more than something to be seen. It represents God's compassion for our humankind in this tempest-tossed world. More than a symbol, it is an experience.

Without that experience we are lost.

INTRODUCING THE ESSAY

Christianity is the only major religion whose founder was executed. Confucius, Moses and Muhammed died natural deaths. The Buddha died accidentally of food poisoning. Shintoism, Taoism and Hinduism have no single founder.

I still wonder how Christianity survived Jesus' death and the disputed reports of his return. I wonder how the early church survived the hatred and persecution of its enemies, the divisions within local churches and the bitter debates among its leaders.

Through all of its existence the church has endured the worldliness, faithlessness and even violence of bishops, pastors, preachers, priests and popes. Catholics, Protestants and Orthodox alike have at times allied themselves with the ruling powers. Such alliances led to the Crusades, the Inquisition, pogroms against Jews, the burning of "heretical" Christians, and unholy wars of Christians against Christians and non-Christians alike. Last year the bishop and priests of the Russian Orthodox Church supported Putin's cruel invasion of the Ukraine. When the church acts like this, one need not wonder why so many leave it.

Despite these betrayals some priests, popes, preachers, pastors and people kept the faith and lived the faith. They showed this in both their prayers and their compassion for the victims of disasters, injustice and violence.

But how did they do this? What kept their faith alive?

In retirement I've been learning more about the faith in which I was raised, which I once abandoned and now gives meaning to my life. Christianity lives today because of Jesus' teachings, healings, miracles and examples.

But there's more in this. What he did during his last three years on earth came to a focus in his last three *days*. That final fraction of his life created a new proclamation of God's compassion for our faltering humanity. It created a community which lived God's compassion.

Christian worship focuses on those three days: Good Friday, Holy Saturday and Easter Sunday, called Pascha in the Eastern churches.

This essay explores his last three days and their impact on uncounted Christians, seekers and non-Christians. This impact, unpredictable and unexpected, is as much the subject of this exploration as well as the three days themselves. I invite you to take this journey with me.

HOW THE CROSS CAME OUT OF THE CRUCIFIXION

Crucifixion

Jewish law directed death by stoning or beheading for certain crimes, but never crucifixion. Jewish law allowed the corpse of executed criminals to be hung on a tree during the day. "If someone is convicted of a crime punishable by death, and is executed, and you hang him on a tree, his corpse must not remain all night on the tree. You shall bury him on the same day, *for anyone hung on a tree is under God's curse*." (Deuteronomy 21: 22–23)

Romans, not Jews, crucified their enemies. The Romans learned it from the Phoenicians, but instead of hanging the body on a tree, as the Phoenicians did, the Romans nailed the offender to a crossbar. They raised the crossbar to the top of a ten-foot stake planted in the ground, and lashed it there. The word "cross" is our translation of a Greek word meaning "stake." The Jehovah's Witness bible calls the cross "the torture stake."

The Romans had several means of execution, but they crucified those who challenged their authority or rebelled against it. Roman citizens, like St. Paul, were exempt from crucifixion. They could be dealt with in other ways.

When Jesus was a young man, a certain Judas in Galilee led a rebellion which the local Roman garrison quickly suppressed. They crucified the surviving rebels and hung their bodies along the road from Nazareth to Capernaum. When walking on that road, Jesus must have seen their dead or dying bodies as a warning to all passers by.

The crucified died slowly and painfully. As long as the victim could hold himself erect, he could breathe. When utterly exhausted, sometimes after hours, his body sank, his head snapped forward and he choked to death.

Crucifixion was a shameful death, exposing the victim's naked body to the spectators. The first Christians felt this shame when considering the crucifixion of Jesus. They must have wondered why Paul spoke and wrote so often and so openly about this ghastly, shameful death. For example, Paul wrote to the church in Galatia: "Christ redeemed us from the curse of the law by becoming a curse for us – for it is written *cursed is everyone who hangs from a tree*."(Galatians 3:13) To the church in Philippi he wrote, "Christ became obedient to the point of death – even death on a cross." (Philippians 2: 7–8.) In Hebrews 12:2 we read "... Jesus ... for the joy that was set before him endured the cross, disdaining the shame."

Jesus' Journey To The Cross

The first four books in the Christian scriptures describe the life and ministry of Jesus. We call them gospels, the English translation of a Greek word meaning "good news."

The gospels do not give us a biography of Jesus or a history of his work as we use those words today The authors wrote to testify that Jesus of Nazareth was not just a great teacher, healer and exemplar, but the Son of Man predicted by the prophets and the Son of God sent by God.

By the time the gospels were written almost everyone who knew Jesus personally had died. But those who had seen and heard him reported their encounters to other Christians who wrote down their reports. These written reports circulated in fragments among the young churches and were then compiled into longer documents. The gospel writers used these longer documents to tell their story. Written in different locations, at different times and from different perspectives, these gospel narratives and, of course, the letters became the written resource for the young church's faith.

The gospels tell us that Jesus was born and raised in Nazareth in the northern province of Galilee. He grew up as a practicing Jew, studying the Torah and prophets, and daily praying the psalms at the local synagogue. Since the gospels say nothing of his father after age twelve, Jesus the eldest son, may have taken up his father's trade and supported the family.

Around the age of thirty he left home to hear his cousin, John, who was preaching at the Jordan river in Judea. Crowds from Jerusalem and Jericho were gathering to hear John's call to repentance and receive his ritual washing in the river. Jesus also was washed, that is baptized, by him.

Filled then with God's spirit, Jesus walked from the river into the Judean desert, where he faced three temptations, and emerged oblivious to home, family, work and neighbors. He became a traveling teacher, healing the lame, the sick, the blind and the possessed, feeding the hungry with bread and belief.

Crowds came to hear him and see his healings, but those who followed him were few, twelve men and some women, all from Galilee. They traveled with him, first through their own province, then south into less-friendly Judea. The women may have paid for their food and lodging.

If Jesus had stuck to preaching and healing, he'd have been safe. But he began to prophesy a huge eruption in history. He announced a new world where the meek and the merciful, peacemakers and the persecuted, the humble and the hungry, would become its citizens. In that world the privileged and powerful would learn the wisdom of the dispossessed.

The Temple priests in Jerusalem and the local teachers of the law soon heard what Jesus was preaching. His prophecy of a new world troubled the priests. His teachings troubled the teachers. His claim to be God's spokesman was blasphemy to both.

Jesus must have realized that if he continued to prophesy God's coming kingdom, the Temple priests would complain to Pilate. Pilate would never tolerate a madman whose preaching might inflame an already rebellious people.

At some point Jesus must have realized that God was asking more from him than sermons and healings. God was asking for his life. Suddenly Jesus gave up healings and feedings. He preached more urgently. He threatened his enemies. He challenged his disciples. Impatient with them, he exploded: "Why are you afraid?" "Why are your hearts so hard?" "Why don't you understand?" "Why have you so little faith?" He frightened and confused them.

Three times he told his disciples he would suffer and be killed, but they didn't believe him. Approaching Jerusalem, he told them this was the city where prophets died. But they didn't believe him.

When he asked his disciples who they thought he was, only Peter answered, "You are the anointed one, the Messiah." When Jesus said he would die in Jerusalem, Peter said, "This will never happen to you." Jesus rebuked him: "Get behind me, you tempter. You're not on God's side." Even Peter, the founder of the church, didn't believe him

While Jesus waited for his inevitable arrest in the olive grove, his disciples fell asleep. When the Temple guard arrived, all but Peter took to their heels. At the trial in the Temple Peter denied three times that he knew Jesus. Then he too ran away.

All the disciples had heard his teachings. All had seen his healings and his miracles. But at the approach of his death, they disappeared. Why? The answer, I think, is clear. *They didn't know who he was.*

They didn't realize that he was not called to lead a rebellion against Rome, but to suffer, die and then live. Only through the crucifixion and only through the mystery of his resurrection could his disciples and eventually the church itself, realize that through him God's incarnate compassion was coming *in person* to a failed humanity.

The Crucifixion of Jesus

The gospels devote one seventh of their text to the last day in Jesus' life. They tell the same story but with variations. Only Matthew describes Judas's suicide. Only Mark describes a naked young man running from the Temple guard. Only in Luke does Jesus appear before Herod. Only John describes Jesus washing the feet of his disciples.

In Mark and Matthew his last words are "My God, my God, why have you forsaken me?" In Luke he says, "Father, into your hands I commend my spirit." In John he says, "It has been accomplished."

With these and other variations, the gospels describe the same seven scenes.

1. Jesus and the disciples celebrate the Passover in a rented second floor room.

2. Jesus and the disciples go to a grove of olive trees outside the city walls. Jesus prays while his disciples sleep. Judas betrays him and the Temple police arrest him. The disciples vanish.

3. At the Temple the high priest interrogates Jesus, accuses him of blasphemy, and sends him to Pilate.

4. Pilate interrogates Jesus at his headquarters. He accedes to the crowd's demand that Jesus be crucified and releases a criminal in his place. Soldiers take Jesus to the guardhouse where they whip and mock him.

5. Then they lead Jesus through the streets of Jerusalem to the execution site outside the city walls. Jesus carries the crossbar for part of the way, but collapses and the soldiers force a passerby, Simon of Cyrene, to carry it from there.

6. At the execution site called Golgotha ("the skull") the soldiers crucify Jesus between two other victims. He dies at mid-afternoon on the day of Passover.

7. A wealthy follower of Jesus, Joseph of Arimathea, gets Pilate's permission to take his body and bury it in his family tomb.

You will find the full narrative in Matthew 26:20–27:66; Mark 14:10–15:47; Luke 22:1–23:56; or John 13:1–10 and 18:1–19:42.

I call your attention to three features in these accounts.

First. In contrast to a current film which spends over twenty minutes on the flogging of Jesus the gospels describe his suffering briefly. The Temple guards slap and hit him. The soldiers in the guardhouse scourge him with a leather whip. After the flogging they march Jesus to the site of execution. On the cross he struggles to stay alive, but collapses and dies.

Even deeper than his pain must have been his despair. Not only his disciples but his God had left him to die alone. Small wonder that he cried from the cross, "My God, my God, why have you abandoned me?" Jesus, God's own Son, was one of us, as mortal in death as in life.

Second. To this day many Christians still believe that Jews killed Jesus. And why? Because the gospels describe Pilate as a *reluctant* executioner. He tells the Temple priests, "I find no crime in this man." He asks the crowds shouting for his blood, "What evil has he done?" He washes his hands saying, "I am innocent of this man's blood," while the crowds cry "His blood be upon us and on our children." He releases a convicted rebel, Barabbas, in place of Jesus."

In contrast to the gospels Pilate's contemporaries describe him as anything but kind. Philo, the Jewish philosopher, wrote, "He was cruel and his hard heart had no compassion. His reign was one of bribery, violence, robbery, misery, oppression, executions without fair trial and infinite cruelty." The historian Josephus reports Pilate's brutal indifference to Jewish faith. He deliberately provoked riots by bringing pigs into the Temple.

Why then do the Gospels try to exculpate Pilate and blame the Jews?

To the Jews Christians were heretics, claiming that in Jesus the Messiah had arrived. To Christians Jews were faithless, denying that God would save the world through Jesus. There could be no compromise The battle of words became a battle of blood, namely the blood of Jews spilled through centuries of violence and suffering.

Jews under pagan Rome enjoyed a special status. Julius Caesar made Judaism a legal religion and exempted Jews from offering the pinch of incense before the emperor's statue. Christians, as members of a new and rather strange religion, were required to make this offering. Those who refused were executed. Anxious to avoid unwanted danger, Christian writers of the crucifixion story tried to reduce Rome's suspicion of their new religion by making Jews the responsible party and Pilate, the well-meaning, but reluctant agent of the mob's rage against Jesus.

The seeds of emnity between Jews and Christians were sewn from the beginning. This early emnity gave birth to countless crucifixions, a few committed by Romans, but most of them by Christians against Jews as well as pagans and each other.

Third. It is important to note that when the Temple police arrived to arrest Jesus in the garden, all his disciples but Peter fled. Peter stayed to watch his trial before the priests before he fled and hid.

And who did go to the cross ? The women: first, the four Marys – Mary his mother, Mary of Magdala, Mary the wife of Clopas and Mary the mother of James and Joses. Others went to the cross with them – the mother of the

Zebedee brothers, a woman named Salome and the women who followed him from Galilee. In the first three gospels the women were the last at the cross and first at the tomb. They witnessed his death. They announced his resurrection.

On women such as these and on men like the disciples rested the future of Jesus' life, message and mission.

The First Witness To The Cross

The four gospels tell the story of Jesus' ministry. Since they are the first books listed in the Christian scriptures and because they describe his life they seem to be the earliest Christian writings. They are not. Scholars estimate that Mark appeared between 65 and 70 CE, Matthew between 70 and 100, Luke between 80 and 100, and John between 90 and 100.

The earliest New Testament writings are Paul's letters written between 50 and 60 C.E. to five young congregations: Corinth and Thessalonica in Greece, Colossus and Galatia in Asia Minor, and Rome. He also wrote to his colleagues, Timothy and Titus, and a Christian slave owner named Philemon.

In his letters to the five churches Paul greets, encourages, admonishes and instructs new Christians in the beliefs and practice of their new-found faith. Paul names other missionaries: Apollos, Barnabas, Cleopas and Timothy, who may also have written letters. Only Paul's survived.

His letters so impacted those five churches just named that they made copies which they sent to other congregations who passed them on to even other churches. By 150 C.E. Paul's letters were being read with the gospels at Christian services. His letters had become scripture.

Paul was qualified to translate a faith which emerged from Judaism and reached the entire Greco-Roman world. Born a Jew and a Roman citizen, Paul grew up in Tarsus, a city ruled by Rome and steeped in Hellenistic culture. He was trilingual and bicultural. He spoke Aramaic at home, Hebrew in the synagogue and Greek in public. He was at ease with his family, his fellow worshippers and his friends in the street and the forum.

As a young man Paul was brilliant, ambitious, and advanced beyond his peers in mastering Jewish tradition. Outraged at Jews who converted to Christianity, he joined a group of zealous colleagues who hunted and harassed these apostates. He admitted to the Christians in Galatia: "I persecuted the church of God violently and tried to destroy it" (1:13).

What might have been a lifetime career came to a halt in 45 C.E., ten or more years after Jesus' crucifixion. Paul had a sudden, personal and powerful encounter with a presence whom he knew instantly to be the source and center of the very faith which he was persecuting. He had met the risen Jesus.

The book of Acts gives the best known account of his conversion. In 9:1–9. Paul (called Saul here) is walking to Damascus, "breathing threats and murder against the disciples." A dazzling light blinds him and he hears a voice asking, "Why do you persecute me?" Paul asks who speaks and the voice says, "Jesus whom you persecute." The voice sends him to Damascus where Christians welcome him.

His sight returns. This account was written at least twenty five years after Paul's actual conversion. Paul himself says nothing of such a meeting. Only once did he describe his encounter with the risen Jesus. To the Christians in Corinth he wrote, "I know a person in Christ who fourteen years ago was caught up in third heaven – whether in the body or out of the body I do not know; God knows – and he was caught up in Paradise and heard things that are not to be told." (II C 12:1–5.)

Paul says that he owed his conversion to no human source. " I did not confer with any human being nor did I go to Jerusalem to visit the apostles." (Galatians 2: 16–17.) After this encounter he says he spent three years alone in Arabia (present day Jordan) and only then did he go to Jerusalem. There he visited Peter and Jesus' brother James, by then the two leaders of the church. After their meeting they confirmed that Paul was an apostle, namely one whose message came directly from Jesus.

Paul wrote to the Christians in Corinth that Jesus "appeared first to Cephas (Peter), then to the twelve disciples and more than five hundred brothers and sisters (see Acts 2:1–16), then to James (the brother of Jesus), then to all the apostles, and finally, as to one untimely born, he appeared to me" (I Cor. 15:6–8).

His confrontation with Christ was not just a mystical moment. It was a life changer. The word went out that "The man who once persecuted us now proclaims the faith he tried to destroy." (Galatians 2:23). Churches began to accept Paul as an apostle.

His new life was no bed of roses. He tells us he was stoned once, shipwrecked three times, flogged nine times and often imprisoned. He added: "I have been constantly on the move. I have been in danger from rivers, danger from bandits, danger from my fellow Jews, danger from Gentiles, danger in the city, danger in the country, danger at sea, and danger from false believers. I have labored and toiled and often gone without sleep. I have known hunger and thirst and gone without food. I have been cold and naked. And besides everything else, I daily face the pressure of my concern for all the churches. Who is weak and I am not weak? Who is made to stumble and I am not indignant?" (II Corinthians 11: 26–28)

What drove Paul in this life-consuming work? From his letters it seems he read nothing of the message and ministry of Jesus. He tells us that what empowered him was the crucifixion and resurrection. His old self had been crucified, a new self resurrected.

He wrote of the resurrection in I Corinthians 15. But more often he wrote of the cross and crucifixion – not as a tragedy to be mourned but a gift to be celebrated.

Paul found forgiveness in the cross. Given the pain which he had inflicted on Christians, Paul could have spent the rest of his life paralyzed by guilt. But he didn't. When he speaks of being forgiven, he is thanking God who had not excused him for his past, but freed him *from* his past. God freed him for a guilt-free future, free to build up the faith and people whom he once tried to destroy.

Guilt paralyzes. Forgiveness liberates.

In the crucifixion Paul saw God reaching out to our entire failing, faltering, dying humanity. God came and comes to the world in One who walks *toward* death, *into* death and *through* death to live the love which death could not and can never conquer.

In his last letter, written to the church in Rome, he calls his fellow Christians "more than conquerors through him who loved us." He writes, "I am convinced that neither death, nor life, nor angels, nor rulers, nor things present, nor things to come, nor height, nor depth, not anything in all creation can separate us from the love of God which is in Christ Jesus our Lord." (8:38–39)

The beauty of nature did not create this faith. Human affection could not create it. Nor could eloquent preaching or elegant writing. Healings, miracles, even threats of death, doom, and damnation did not then and cannot now change the human heart. It took and still takes a life, a human life that was and is and always will be God's life among us.

The Cross And The First Christians

The church was already growing before Paul began his work. In Jerusalem, Antioch, Haifa and other cities in Palestine and Syria small groups of Christians were gathering to pray, read scripture and share their faith. Paul and his colleagues found these people waiting for someone to deepen their faith and shape their practice of it.

These converts lived in a cold, corrupt world, ruled by Rome and its minions – governors, tax collectors, informers and army. Christian converts found the gods of Greece and Rome remote and their philosophies a distant comfort. The new faith caught their imaginations and touched their hope for something more than bread and circuses. This new counter-cultural religion pointed people to a transcendent life which they desperately needed.

Paul described the situation in words which I've rephrased: "The masses want miracles and the intellectuals want philosophy, but we preach Christ crucified, a stumbling block to some and foolishness to the others, but to those of us who hear God's call, the crucified Christ is the power of God and the wisdom of God." (see I Corinthians 1:21–22.)

True then, true now.

Holy Communion
Celebrates The Crucifixion

From its beginning, Holy Communion was and still is today the primary form of worship for most Christians. Its Greek name,"eucharist," means "thanksgiving." It is a service composed of mostly words but the words point forward to an *action* – the worshipers' reception of the consecrated elements, the bread and wine. Through them they receive Christ's presence.

Twenty years after the crucifixion Christians were celebrating communion. The first mention of it appears in Paul's letter to the Christians in Corinth. He had heard that their observance of the Eucharist had turned into a free-for-all and he wrote to rebuke them.

Paul wrote, "When you gather together, it is not really to eat the Lord's Supper. For when the time comes to eat, each of you goes ahead with his own meal, and one goes hungry and another gets drunk. What? Do you not have your own homes to eat and drink in? Will you despise the church of God and humiliate those who have nothing? What shall I say? Shall I commend you for such behavior? I will not." (I Cor. 11: 20–22)

Then Paul instructs them: "For I received *from the Lord* what I also passed on to you, namely that the Lord Jesus on the night when he was betrayed, took bread, and when he had given thanks, he broke it and said, 'This is my body which is for you' (that is, on your behalf). In the same way he took the cup after supper saying, 'This is the new covenant in my blood. Do this in remembrance (or re-enactment) of me.'" (I Cor. 11:23–26)

These words, written by Paul in 55 C.E., appear in the gospels fifteen to fifty years later. In Matthew's and Mark's accounts of the Last Supper, Jesus says "This is the blood of the covenant which is poured out for many." Matthew adds "For the forgiveness of sins." In all three gospels Jesus says that he will not drink of the fruit of the vine until he drinks it in the kingdom of God. In Luke he blesses the cup before the bread. In all three accounts he says of the bread, "This is my body."

In our time priests and pastors repeat some form of these words, when giving the consecrated elements to the people. A Catholic priest might say "The body of Christ" and "The blood of Christ." An Episcopal priest might say, "The body of Christ, the bread of heaven" and "The blood of Christ, the cup of salvation." An Orthodox priest says the parishioner's name and adds the words of administration. Protestant churches, based solely on scripture, might quote Paul's words literally. In some churches the pastor says, "Take this in remembrance of Jesus."

The essential words are "the body of Christ" and "the blood of Christ." These words may confuse or offend Christians in our time as they did the first Christians. I must explain them.

Jesus' crucifixion was a grim event. His body broke down during his last three hours and when he could no longer hold himself upright, he choked to death and his body began to decompose.

Christians see more than suffering in this death. Through this suffering they see the mystery and miracle of God's compassion for our humankind. This compassion transformed faithful women and timid disciples into a new community, the seed of the church.

Think of it! The disintegration of a tortured body became the occasion for thanksgiving.

When Paul in his letters wrote, "the body of Christ," he wasn't referring to the corpse of Jesus, but to something quite different. He meant the people who would be reading his letters. He tells them, "You are the body of Christ." He says, "We, though many, are one body in Christ." He calls Christ "the head of the body," The body was and is the church, the fellowship of the faithful.

In the same way the phrase, "the blood of Christ," takes on new meaning. In Greek the word for blood (*aimati*) is synonymous with life. Without blood there is no life.

At the last supper Jesus lifts the cup of Passover wine and says, "This is my life given for you in a new covenant." God's presence through his coming death will be passed on to his followers. That is why Paul says at the end of his instructions, "For as often as you eat this bread and drink this cup, you proclaim the Lord's death until he comes." The people proclaim the death of Jesus because it is a *life-giving death*. Jesus surrenders his earthly blood and body so God's life in him can be released to those who have trusted him.

The church believes that the risen Jesus is present at Holy Communion. How Christ is present is a mystery. I'm going to repeat that. *How* Christ is present in the eucharist is a mystery. And what is a mystery? Something that we know to be true, but cannot explain. The event is true. The explanation almost always fails.

Different Christian traditions do try to explain Christ's presence at the eucharist. What is more important than these attempts and what is common to all is the experience of Christ's presence. Every Sunday all over the world Christians receive Holy Communion, sometimes at risk to their fortunes, security and even lives. But they continue. Why? Because in this ritual they experience the life-giving compassion of God, the life-giving death of His Son and His servants through all time.

Let me give you an example.

In 1957 the new government in China expelled all foreign missionaries and made Christian worship illegal. The government, like Pilate and the priests, thought their authority would end this upstart religion. These actions could not have done more to strengthen the church. Half-hearted Christians abandoned the church, thus cleansing it. The rest took their Christianity underground. They rediscovered their faith in their homes.

Twenty years after the ban my younger brother, about to leave a year of teaching in Tianjin, witnessed this. On his last Sunday in Tianjin a student took him to the first Christian service to be held in that city for twenty years. During this time the church had been turned into a warehouse. As they walked to the church, my brother asked, "How will anyone know where the church is?" The student said, "They will know." My brother asked, "How will they know there *is* a service?" The student said, "They will know."

As they approached the church they could hear the hymn singing a block away. Despite two decades of closures, threats and imprisonments, these homebound Christians had been saying their prayers, reading their scriptures, singing their hymns, teaching their children and receiving Holy Communion, when a priest or pastor visited them. Such was the power of the transcendent compassion which they had received.

Showing The Cross

If Jesus had been executed in our time, he would have been shot, hung or gassed. Imagine entering a church and seeing on the altar a small model of a gallows or gas chamber. It would be a shocker. So was the cross for the first Christians.

For that reason the earliest Christian symbol was not a cross but two letters of the Greek alphabet. Imagine a capital X superimposed on a capital R. In Greek these would be the first two letters of the Greek word, "Christos," meaning "the anointed one," in Hebrew "the Messiah." It was first a title given Jesus which became part of his name, Jesus Christ. Since kings and priests were ordained to their office by being anointed with oil, so Jews believed the Messiah would be designated. Thus "Jesus Christ" *could* be roughly translated as "Joshua the Designated."

Another early symbol of Jesus was a fish. The letters in the Greek word for fish, "ichthous," form an acrostic in Greek, "Jesus Christ Son of God and Saviour," the first proclamation of Christian faith,

The first Christians painted Jesus. On the walls of their underground graves, the catacombs, we find faded portrayals of him as a shepherd tending his sheep or carrying a lamb. Other paintings show him as the vine which nourishes the branches, his churches. Mosaics in the first Christian basilicas depict him as a king sitting on a throne.

The earliest depiction of the cross itself is a crudely drawn cartoon, dated about 200 CE. It shows a man with the head of a donkey on a cross. Beneath him another man looks up at this figure and lifts a reverent hand toward it. The inscription reads "Alexamenos worships his god." The earliest depiction of the crucifixion mocks the crucifixion.

The earliest Christian depiction of the crucifixion is a carving in ivory. It shows Christ on the cross, calm and composed. His outstretched arms seem to say, "Come to me, you who bear heavy burdens. I will give you rest." At one side of Jesus an enemy shakes his fist at him. At the other side two women look at him with reverence. At the far left the body of Judas hangs from a tree. This carving is dated about 400 C.E.

All of us are familiar with portrayals of Jesus which show him bruised and bleeding, dying or dead, on the cross. Thousands of artists have drawn, painted or sculpted this scene. This scene has been a source of comfort and inspiration to the faithful for over a millennium. Modern painters might connect Christ's suffering with that of exiles, refugees, immigrants, and other victims of oppression or violence.

We find a different kind of portrayal in Eastern Christian homes and churches. Called icons (the Greek word for "image"), these are stylized, semi-abstract representations, showing both the holiness and humanity of the subject Jesus, the Holy Mother or a saint.

The Orthodox icon for Easter Sunday might surprise you. As Catholics and Protestants we have seen depictions of Jesus rising from the tomb, greeting Mary in the garden, eating with his disciples or ascending to heaven. But the Easter (Paschal) icon in the Eastern churches is a stunner. It shows Christ in hell.

That's right – hell.

This hell, however, is not a furnace with pitchforks, fire and boiling oil. Nor is it Dante's icy pit described in the Inferno. This hell is a grey, sad, shadowy world of departed spirits called in Hebrew "Sheol." The psalms describe Sheol as a place without joy or grief, without hope or gratitude, a world where its residents cannot remember God nor can God remember them. (See Psalms 6:5, 28:2, 88:5, 115:17) Christ came into this half-life, say Eastern Christians, after dying on the cross. And why? To save those who are caught in hell!

In the Paschal icon Christ, dressed in white and surrounded by a nimbus of blinding light, stands on the gates of hell, which he has just smashed down. He grasps the wrists of a man on one side and a woman on the other. The man is Adam and the woman is Eve. Adam and Eve are us, caught in our own hells, stuck in our personal sins, the sins we chose and the sins we were born into (our collective sins of nation, race, culture, class, gender and religion.)

At one side a small group looks on: David the legendary king of Israel, his son Solomon, John the Baptist, and the prophets. These people are in hell not because they were bad but because they weren't Christians. They hadn't been baptized.

The story says that before Christ rose from the grave, before he appeared to Mary and his disciples, before he ascended to heaven, he knew that he must rescue everyone caught hell but in order to reach these souls he must die. That's why he courted death on the cross and instead of going straight to heaven burst into hell and lifted Eve and Adam and all humanity, non-Christians included, into the light of God's presence.

I called this a story. By doing so I do not demean but elevate its truth. Story and history are two ways of seeing the world. Northrup Frye says, "History tells us what happened. Story tells us what always happens." The story of Christ entering hell is always happening.

Think of those in our day who enter this world's hells in order to help humanity: journalists on dangerous truth-seeking assignments; men and women risking bombs, disease and their own fear to heal the sick and wounded in war-torn countries; therapists who risk their own peace of mind to listen the suffering out of others; and priests, monks, nuns and others who leave the comfort of their homelands to spend the rest of their lives with peoples in impoverished countries.

If I cannot do what they do, I can be thankful for what they do. For me these people, Christians or non-Christians, re-enact Christ entering hell to save the lost and the forgotten.

Enacting The Cross

Crosses are not just drawn, painted and sculpted. They are enacted too.

1. The simplest enactment is crossing oneself. As early as 300 C.E. a church father wrote, "On our journeys, on our going in and coming out, at our sitting down and putting on our shoes, at meals, at the kindling of lights, at baths and bedtime, at whatever occupation engages us, we mark the brow with the sign of the cross."

    Crossing oneself is an essential act in Catholic and Orthodox liturgies and devotions. Outside of churches, though, we rarely see this act except at funerals or burials or perhaps at the bed of a loved one whose life hangs between life and death.

2. Another enactment is wearing a cross as a pendant around the neck or attached to the lapel of a suit jacket. Given the recent popularity of this symbol, one sometimes cannot know whether it's a sign of faith or fashion.

3. A rare enactment of the cross is the stigmata. Two years before his death St. Francis of Assisi became the first Christian on whose hands and feet the signs of Christ's crucifixion appeared. Since then a few of the faithful have shown these signs, most recently a Capuchin priest, Padre Pio, who died in 1968.

4. A more dramatic enactment of the crucifixion began after World War II in the Philippines among a people with a deep tradition of folk religion and Catholic Christianity. On Good Friday certain candidates re-enact Christ's crucifixion. They do this in repentance for a grievous sin or in thanksgiving for a blessing. A Danish stunt man did it to find the God in whom he didn't believe. He tells us he found God. Or, perhaps God found him.

5. Pilgrimages are journeys to a cross in a distant church or chapel. Some of the faithful carry heavy crosses on the way. Others make the journey on blood-stained knees. The Camino, a walk from Portugal or France to the cathedral of St. James in Santiago, is an ancient and still popular tradition. Some walk for exercise, some for achievement, some to kick a bad habit, some to deepen their life with God. Churches and chapels along the way and the great altar in the Santiago cathedral remind these pilgrims of Christ's sacrifice which may bless theirs. Some of my Unitarian Universalist colleagues have walked the Camino.

6. Singing is another way to enact the cross. At King's Chapel I heard the choir sing King John of Portugal's setting of the "Crux Fidelis." I grew up among a people who sang such hymns as "The Old Rugged Cross," "When I survey the wondrous cross" and "In the cross of Christ I glory." When we were interned during World War II we sang these hymns on the ball field on Sunday evenings. I sing them still.

Living The Cross

How do we live the cross? That's a serious question.

Shall we emulate our favorite heroes and heroines? Ghandi? Dietrich Bonhoeffer? Oscar Romero? Martin Luther King? Edith Stein? Or our local saints who cared for the poor in Boston: Paul Sullivan, Kip Tiernan, Barbara McGinnis, John Leary, Jim O'Connell and my dear, deceased friend, Jed Mannis? In comparison with these people I feel small and grateful.

These people lived in Christian communities which lived God's love and this empowered them to spend themselves for others. What they received they could not help but give. Their gifts came not from guilt, but gratitude.

For me this means that when I live deeply into the life of a faith community, I will be moved by God's compassion. When I open myself to that compassion, I will be guided to do what I can do. When I pray for others, write a check, give a dollar to a friend on the street, phone or write a letter to someone in trouble; when I write this text, try to listen to the pain of my friends, or let myself feel sad at their suffering; when I do these things. I may be sharing what I've been given.

A Warning: The Cross Corrupted

The cross can be abused.

Only three centuries after the crucifixion Constantine marched his army toward Rome with a large army, intent on taking the city and with it the Roman empire. His opponent, Maxentius, waited for him in the city.

Before the final battle the historian Eusebius reports that Constantine had a vision of a cross with a bright light shining around it. The message to Constantine was clear: "In this sign you shall conquer." He had the emblem painted on the shields of his soldiers and in the ensuing battle defeated Maxentius and became emperor.

Christians have told and retold this story for centuries as proof of God's blessing on the emerging church. And why shouldn't they? Once in power Constantine gave to the church the same freedom which other religions enjoyed. He restored to the church properties taken by earlier administrations. He made Sunday the official day of rest. He built impressive churches in Rome, Jerusalem and Bethlehem. He transferred the capital of his new empire from Rome to Byzantium, a small Christian city in Asia Minor. He renamed it Constantinople, and just before he died he was baptized.

During his reign Constantine took no action against Jews and pagans, but his successors did. Christian emperors soon imposed on non-Christians the same restrictions which were once imposed on Christians. Christian bishops pressed state officials to make life difficult for Jews and pagans. They also attacked Christians who failed to obey their commands. The first Christian to be killed for heresy was Priscillian, the leader of a small Christian sect in Spain. In 386 C.E. he and five followers were executed at the order of the Spanish bishops.

Horrors followed: the papal army's slaughter of the Waldensians on the slopes of the Alps; the Crusaders' destruction of Constantinople; the Protestant persecution of the Anabaptists; Queen Mary's persecution of the Protestants in England and her sister Elizabeth's persecutions of Catholics; the St. Bartholomew's Day massacre of Protestants in France; the Jesuit destruction of the Polish Unitarian church, and countless other acts of violence committed in the name of Christ.

All this is nothing compared to the church's persecution of non-Christians: the Crusaders' butchery of Muslims in the Holy Land; the Inquisition's persecution of the Jews; church and state pogroms against Jews in Poland and Russia; the church's abduction and reprogramming of native children in the United States, Canada and Australia; the church's support for slavery and racism, and its silence during local lynchings in the South.

To these we must add the European church's war on the religion and culture of the native peoples in the Americas and Australia. Christian armies massacred or enslaved the Maya and Aztec peoples of Mexico, Bolivia and Peru. All this and more can happen when the church marries the state and becomes its agent.

Sometimes individual Christians acted directly. Jews in Europe feared Good Friday, when Christian mobs, inflamed by preachers at the morning Mass, attacked their homes and sometimes burned them in their synagogues. What are the swastika and the flaming emblems of the Ku Klux Klan, but the cross burned and twisted as an instrument of murderous intent?

The church should mourn, not celebrate, Constantine's vision of the cross as the sign in which he would conquer. At that point the sign of God's compassion became an emblem of brutal power.

A Russian exile in Paris denounced this perversion of Christianity. Nicholas Berdyaev, once a Marxist and supporter of the revolution, became a Christian, then a priest among his fellow emigres in France. In exile he wrote: "Truth nailed to the cross compels nobody, oppresses no one. It must be accepted and confessed freely. Its appeal is addressed to free spirits. ... A divine Truth panoplied in power, triumphant over the world and conquering souls, would not be consonant with the freedom of man's spirit. The mystery of Golgotha is the mystery of liberty ... Every time in history that humankind has tried to turn the crucified Truth into the coercive truth it has betrayed the fundamental principle of Christ."

A Woman Who Lived The Cross

On May 8, 1373, the third Sunday after Easter, a thirty-one year old woman lay unconscious and feverish in her parents' house in Norwich, England. Devout from her youth she had prayed to experience Christ's crucifixion, to receive his wounds and to suffer intense illness. Fearful for her life her parents called the priest who held the crucifix before her eyes and prayed for her.

After five hours of feverish struggle the young woman laughed aloud and slowly returned to consciousness. She recovered her health and continued her usual duties and devotions at home. During this time she wrote an account of the fifteen visions of Christ's crucifixion which had come to her during this illness.

At the age of thirty-nine she asked the bishop for permission to live as an anchoress at her local church, St. Julian's, in Norwich. He gave her permission, and the saint's name. She was lodged in a small room attached to the church, a room with three windows. Through one which opened onto the sanctuary she received Holy Communion. Through another she received food and passed out slops to the maid who assisted her. The third window opened onto King Street, the main thoroughfare in Norwich. Through that window she counseled those who came to her for comfort, counsel and prayer.

At age fifty-one she wrote a second account of her visions four times longer than the first. This document lay unread until a French monk found it in his abbey's library. You can find online several versions of this text in English, titled *Showings (or Revelations) of Divine Love.*

In these texts Julian described her vision of Christ's suffering on the cross: "I saw the body bleeding copiously, the blood hot, flowing freely, a living stream … and I saw this in the furrows made by his scourging;" and later, "I saw his sweet face dry and bloodless, pale and languishing, the pallor turning blue, as death took hold upon his flesh."

She describes more of this agony in descriptions worthy of a painting by El Greco or Gruenewald. What may baffle the modern reader is Julian's interpretation of her visions. Much as she laments her Savior's suffering, much more she gives thanks for God's love in Christ's self-sacrifice. The further we read through the account of her visions the more jubilant she becomes, rejoicing in God's victory over sin and death.

We might dismiss Julian's optimism as an escape into a dream world of hope and fantasy. But we must remember that through her window onto King Street Julian saw and heard the suffering, violence, cruelty and disasters afflicting the people of her city. She heard the anxiety of farmers whose cattle had died in droves and others trying to survive the worst harvest in Norwich history. Three outbreaks of the black death killed thousands of its citizens. When the linen industry failed in Flanders across the English channel, so did flax farming around Norwich. The economy never recovered.

Through her window Julian watched rebellious peasants surge through King Street, butchering their enemies. A few days later through the same window she watched the bishop's army slaughter the rebels. Throughout these larger dramas came the never-ending line of Norwich wives and mothers with their accounts of abusive husbands, dying infants, sickness or starvation at home, perhaps their loss of faith as well.

Julian encouraged all who came to her. She speaks of Christ's "royal friendship" and adds "I saw plainly that our Lord was never angry nor ever could be." "Our courteous Lord wills that we should be at home with him." She assured her listeners, "Do not accuse yourself too much or think your distress is all your fault. You will experience distress whatever you do."

She said, "Our good Lord spoke quietly, 'You will not be overcome.' He did not say 'You will not have a rough passage.' He did not say 'You will never be over strained.' He did not say 'You will never be uncomfortable.' But he did say 'You will never be overcome.'" What she wrote in her journal must be what she told the people who came to her window.

These few quotes barely hint at the depth of her faith. I've taught Julian three times. I've read and reread her journal and I'm still scratching the surface. I was pleased to read Julian's challenge to church dogma on salvation: "Everything is included in the mankind who are to be saved, everything that has been created. I speak of those who are to be saved and God has showed me nothing else." She was a universalist before the word was known.

When Julian mourned for those who would suffer in hell, God said to her, "What is impossible for you is not impossible for me. I shall keep my word in everything and everything shall be well." Then followed that splendid mantra, "All shall be well, and all shall be well, and all manner of things shall be well."

That's good news, if I ever heard it, and it came from her visions of Christ dying on the cross.

(above) The five letters of the Greek word for fish form an acrostic which represents the earliest confession of Christian faith: "Jesus Christ Son of God and Savior." A fish drawn on parchment, dirt or the palm of one's hand was an early Christian symbol.

(above) This cartoon mocks a Christian worshipping the cross. It is the earliest known depiction of the crucifixion, dated 200 AD. The inscription reads "Alexander worships his god."

(right) This early crucifix carved in ivory shows a strong, assertive Jesus on the cross. Dated 400 AD.

(below) What does Jesus say to His Father?" Forgive them?" "Why have you abandoned me?" "Into your hands I commit my spirit?"

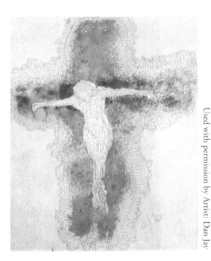

(above) This crucifix which hangs in my study shows Jesus on the cross, but is he dying or dancing?

This cross made of nails bears witness to the crucifixion. It hangs in the chapel of St. Barnabas Church in Falmouth, MA.

This watercolor created by Dan Jay represents the death of Jesus as an almost mystical event.

INTRODUCTION TO THE RESPONSES

After I finished the last draft of this essay it
seemed incomplete, a soliloquy waiting to
become a conversation. I sent the text to some
friends and colleagues and asked them to read
and respond to what I'd written.

Fifteen responded.
They came from differing Christian traditions
plus one Buddhist. They include a park ranger,
a therapist, a hospice chaplain, a journalist,
a university professor, a devotee of Henry David
Thoreau, a survivor of a near-fatal stroke,
one parish minister, five retired clergy
and a writer of murder mysteries.

I hope you will read their responses,
not just for what they learned from the essay
but from their own lives as well.

KATE BAKER CARR

Just as Carl Scovel's ministry has blessed many for more than six decades, his recent article blesses us with the invitation to ponder again and anew how the cross came out of the crucifixion. Scovel's exploration of the historical facts surrounding the crucifixion and the events that followed reminds us that while we can agree on facts, we ascend to Truth.

The article contains an essential and often-overlooked reminder "It was the Romans who crucified their enemies." Down through history and to this day, far too many people hold Jews responsible for the death of Jesus and seek direct or indirect retribution. The article points out that "Jews in Europe feared Good Friday when Christian mobs, inflamed by preaching at the morning Mass, attacked their homes and sometimes burned whole congregations in their synagogues." In these grim and grave times with anti-Semitism again on the rise, it is essential to recall that the authorities representing the imperial Roman empire crucified Jesus, "a criminal who preached sedition and threatened the Pax Romana." Christianity and anti-Semitism are antithetical.

The article importantly warns how easily "the cross can be corrupted and abused." How tragic that Constantine interpreted the vision of "a cross with a bright light shining around it" as a justification for imperial conquest rather than a call to incarnational compassion. The article outlines some of the past horrors that "can happen when the church gains political power. Swastikas and cross burnings remain a part of the landscape. "Christian Democracy" in Hungary and "Christian Nationalism" in the United States are on the rise. These autocratic movements advocate white supremacy, patriarchal domination, and closed borders. Like other corruptions, these movements are a profound betrayal of Jesus' teachings.

The betrayals underscore how critical it is to keep not just *a cross*, but *the cross of Jesus* central to our understanding of the crucifixion.

In the first century, the Roman Empire crucified thousands of freedom fighters and perceived rabble rousers. Why then is Jesus' crucifixion the one among thousands we remember? And why is Jesus' crucifixion essential to Christianity? Would it not be enough to center our faith on Jesus' brave life and prophetic teachings, on his miraculous healings and acts of life-changing mercy? Scovel holds "that Jesus' teachings, healings, miracles and claims to Godness during his last three years on earth were prelude and preparation for his last three days on earth when his ministry came to a focus." Indeed. So too, priest and scholar David Tracy proclaims that "the cross and the resurrection live together or not at all." (Quoted in *Creation and the Cross*, Elizabeth Johnson, p. 104)

The first encounters of the faithful followers and disciples with the Risen Jesus are at once life changing and incredible, so incredible that they had to be seen, even touched, to be believed.

Luke recounts that the first women at the tomb discovered that the stone had been rolled away and the body of Jesus was gone. Two angels reminded the grieving women of all that Jesus told them, including that he must "be delivered into the hands of sinful men and be crucified and on the third day rise. And the women remembered his words, and returning from the tomb they told all this to the eleven and to all the rest. … but these seemed to the disciples and the rest an idle tale and they did not believe the women." (Luke 24:8–12).

The women's truthful witness was too incredible to be believed.

The Gospel of John recounts that "On the evening of that first day of the week ... Jesus came and stood among the disciples and said, 'Peace be with you!' After he said this, he showed them his hands and side." (John 20:19–20)

Thomas, who was not with them, found the disciples' truthful witness too incredible be believed.

Thomas stated "'Unless I see the nail marks in his hands and put my finger where the nails were, and put my hand into his side, I will not believe.' A week later his disciples were in the house again, and Thomas was with them. Though the doors were locked, Jesus came and stood among them and said, 'Peace be with you!' Then he said to Thomas, 'Put your finger here; see my hands. Reach out your hand and put it into my side. Stop doubting and believe.' Thomas said to him, 'My Lord and my God!'" (John 20:25–28).

The Gospels and the Book of Acts reveal that the Risen Jesus was eager to meet his faithful followers and disciples, his apostles and friends, where they were — at the empty tomb, behind a locked door, in a boat, on a road to Emmaus — that they might see and encounter him, that they might believe the incredible. In the first century, Paul encountered Jesus on the road to Damascus. In the thirteenth century, Julian of Norwich encountered Christ in vision-filled dreams. At the close of the twentieth century, in South Hadley, Massachusetts, a 90-year-old woman named Ida Priestly fell by the kitchen table and could not get up. Later that day she recounted to her friend and pastor, the Rev. Gustave Peterson, that "Jesus came to me. He said 'Ida, get up.' So I took his outstretched hand and he helped me to the chair. Then he vanished."

But what of us who "have not seen and yet believe?" (John 20:29b). How does our faith come to life? For some, it can be a gift from others. In Scovel's words, "We can only give what we've been given." In one of her books,

Madeleine L'Engle recounts a wonderful story that goes something like this: When asked why he was a Christian, prominent priest and preacher Phillips Brooks responded: "I am a Christian because of my aunt who lives in Teaneck, NJ." Thank goodness for aunts and all those who pass on what they've been given!

Some come to faith because they themselves experience the agony of crucifixion and, by the grace of God, emerge transformed into the incredible miracle of new life. Has this happened to you? When grief no longer chokes, when illness no longer destroys, when betrayal no longer haunts, when fear no longer binds, when addiction no longer grips, when despair no longer torments, when depression no longer suffocates, when wounds no longer hurt, it is a resurrection.

More than 40 years ago from the pulpit at King's Chapel, Scovel proclaimed words I still hold dear: "Christianity teaches not so much that life comes *after* death but that life comes out of death, big deaths and little deaths, spiritual deaths and physical deaths." When we experience a resurrection on this side of eternity, we encounter the risen Christ. When we experience a resurrection, we ascend to the Truth that the cross of Jesus comes of out the crucifixion not as a sign of death, but as a sign of new life and God's eternal love. Thanks be to God!

MY UNNAMED FRIEND

I have always struggled deeply with the entire idea of the crucifixion, having been taught in my childhood church that we humans are so bad that Jesus had to be tortured and murdered so that we could be acceptable to God. Well, at least that's the message that I heard and carried with me to adulthood. Carl's interpretation of the crucifixion raises ideas that take me down different paths. The crucifixion is embedded in all my questions of why there is so much hatred and suffering in the world that is done by choice, not by happenstance.

The political manipulation, the cruelty, the greed for power, the defining people as "other" that Jesus faced has, throughout human history and into present-day, continues to cause outrageous suffering for people all over the world. Having seen war up close in several locations in Eastern Europe, I am always overwhelmed by the stupidity of it all.

I can understand the intellectual reasons of how propaganda – political or religious – can manipulate beliefs and that facts rarely change beliefs. It seems that we will kill each other over our sense of identity more than anything else. But understanding the "how" does nothing to answer the screaming of "WHY???" that reverberates in my soul.

To think of the crucifixion as an act of compassion aligns more closely with the remarkable courage, sacrifice, and agape love that I have seen firsthand in war zones. During a time of "ethnic cleansing," while safely hidden in some underbrush, I witnessed a man lean down to pick up a young boy standing beside him as they were all about to be shot. They both died. The man's action did nothing to change the outcome. But as he cradled that small boy to his chest, his courage, dignity and compassion completely changed how that terrified boy spent the last few minutes of his life. This man would never know that anyone saw what he did. But I have never forgotten him.

He is one of the greatest examples to me that we always have a choice in how we respond to what is happening, even when we can't change it. He has caused me to often meditate on people who have truly lived Christ's example, be they Christian or not. And while there are many stories where we can name those individuals, I think more often about all the stories we will never know, the silent acts of courage and sacrifice that no one survived to tell but are vitally important to the fabric of the story of humanity. The darker the sky, the brighter the light of the stars; against the darkest of evil. There have always been those people who are pinpoints of brilliant light. To simply remain a decent person in the face of barbarity is an act of love.

While the crucifixion may have more theological implications, that act of compassion and sacrifice for other people has been emulated over and over again, often by the most unlikely of heroes. Christ is in good company.

ANITA FARBER-ROBERTSON

I have never found the cross to be as compelling as the messages Jesus preached by his words and actions. I have been a "follower of Jesus" Christian. So, much of your paper opened inquiries I had not pursued. Thank you.

You offer an accessible understanding of the cross and its meaning. I too have found Julian of Norwich spiritually insightful, though her story is uncomfortable. In response to Julian's visions and her assertion that "All shall be well, and all shall be well, and all manner of things shall be well," you say: "That's good news, if I ever heard it, and it came … from her visions of Christ dying on the cross." My response: *It is good news*, and it tempts me to think it is Julian who is the divine messenger delivering with clarity what had previously been an awkward and very opaque message.

I was deeply touched by your naming the point at which Jesus realizes the depth of God's request of him, namely that God is asking for his life. A powerful awakening. It reminds me of his earlier awakening (Matt. 15, Mk. 7) evoked by the Syrophoenician Woman; suddenly his call extends beyond the House of Israel. It validates my Christian experience when we recognize that Jesus' own spiritual understanding changes and deepens with new encounters, as does my own.

Your calling attention to the political pressures that led the Jews to deny that Christians were Jews, and the Christians to retaliate by denouncing them is surely important. And it is not the whole of it. That they were each claiming to be the favored children of God, the owners of the covenant, made the rivalry existential, not just political. That hasn't stopped.

I appreciated your retelling of Paul's conversion experience. It makes sense as you tell it. If what happened to Paul had happened to me, I would need several years to process and understand it. It was not only life changing, but also identity changing. That takes some time to integrate.

Your presentation of the deeper faith Paul developed is powerful. It was Paul's experience, not his hearing about Jesus' journey through the cross, that brought him to a core experience of divine forgiveness. Your conclusion "The beauty and cycles of nature could not create this kind of faith" (that nothing can separate us from the love of God) rings true. The beauty and cycles of life do evoke transcendence, which is spiritual, but it is not an experience of being loved. You go on, "It took and still takes a life, a human life that was and is a divine life. It took such a life to show us a love above and beyond our good and lesser selves." I am still thinking about that. I would not be comfortable saying that is the only way that God could convey God's love to us, but I could accept that it is the way that God chose and a way we are somewhat able to receive.

Your discussion of communion and the meaning of Paul's words is compelling and extremely helpful. That the gathered community is the current body and blood of Christ, and it is in the name of that corporate body that we partake together of the spiritual sustenance he bequeathed us, not only makes sense, it heals, holds and sustains us. This was a new way for me to hear those words and enter the experience. Thank you.

I am captivated by your discussion of Holy Saturday and the importance of Jesus dying so that he could enter Sheol and bring those souls out to enter into communion with God. It confirms universalism, that proclaims all souls shall be redeemed and reconciled. Before, I professed universalism, having inferred it from the living Jesus' words and example.

Through your presentation, I now can conceive that a loving God would put God's own son through the torture and pain of death to enable him to unlock the door to Sheol, insuring that "neither death, nor life, nor angels, nor rulers, nor things present, nor things to come, nor height, nor depth, not anything else in all creation can separate us from the love of God." (Rom.8:38–39). What a story! Such a gift. Amen.

STEPHEN C. FISHER

Thank you, Carl, for the opportunity to ponder in my heart and engage with this enlightening piece into which you have poured so much of yourself. I am grateful for your offering! I read it as a sort of credo and reclaiming of your Christian heritage in your own distinctive way. While there were a number of reflections I might have included, I am choosing to limit my comments to one of your central themes, that of Living the Cross.

CROSS AND RESURRECTION AS INDIVISIBLE

While you focused on what it means to live the Cross, I would like to view living the Cross and Resurrection as a seamless whole. You write very evocatively that "through this suffering (of Jesus on the Cross), they (Christians) see the mystery and miracle of God's compassion for all humankind, (which) transformed (them) into a new community." While I find this compelling, I doubt that it would have been true for the early Christians had they not beheld the fulfillment of this love in Resurrection. Was it not through this suffering plus the experience of resurrection bursting out from it, this unitive diptych, that this transmutation took place?

Perhaps the early church's experience of Christ's cross born compassion WAS the resurrection, their own resurrection too, perhaps this compassion, this suffering with, was the seedbed, the motive force, the generative power enabling them to perceive its radiance and simultaneously to be grasped by the resurrection. So I see these two experiences of Cross and Resurrection "becoming one flesh," as naturally inseparable as in-breath and out-breath, an indivisible whole. Somehow this "miracle of God's compassion" allowed these nascent Christians to breathe in the sting of death, embrace it wholeheartedly and breathe out new life, such that Jesus was alive again in their midst.

LIVING THE CROSS (AND RESURRECTION)

I would like to comment and expand upon your section on "living the cross" in which you emphasize the importance of living the cross as a way of BEING, as opposed to a DOING, where you stress that the "passive," receptive mode is critical for the gift of the cross to come alive for us, animating our being. You make the critically important point that there are no strings attached to God's compassion, that it is an utterly gratuitous gift that we need only accept and trust. I expect you'd agree that this necessitates a process of humbling ourselves, admitting that we are fundamentally "weak" human beings, following the example of Christ described by St Paul where "he emptied himself, taking the form of a slave." Receiving can certainly require that much humility! Then out of this deep need, we may be led to courageously open ourselves to the great mystery of the cross, God's tender embrace.

You affirm that to live the Cross means receiving this "offer of God's compassion for each of us as we are." You suggest that we can come to know this compassion directly in ritual gestures such as prayer, communion and simply being in the presence of the Holy One who loves us without condition. You further suggest that we can encounter and come to know this compassion through the "saving acts" of those who have modeled this compassion for us, those who have loved us, sacrificed for us, overlooked the fool in us, been present to us and truly seen us, seen us without judging us in all our goodness and brokenness. If we receive, live with and truly companion the "One who walks toward, into and through death," if we receive this gift of life, of love, as Jacques Brel proclaimed in song:

"Love that's falling like rain
Then our parched desert earth, will grow green again.
If we only have love, then Jerusalem stands,
and then death has no shadow, there are no foreign lands."

A real challenge in life is to allow the love offered us to be taken in, to be fully received. As Bede Griffith, the Benedictine monk and mystical writer once commented, what we are often most afraid of in life is not rejection or judgment but daring to accept that we are loved, a gesture that can dissolve all of our ego controls and leave us naked and vulnerable as was Jesus on the Cross. As you have observed, it is only in daring to open to this transformation of our inner being in love that can allow us, in turn, to act out of love and gratitude, not guilt. So this receiving is most often a priori to our being able to give authentically to others and the world.

But I believe that it can also be true that BEING and DOING need not be opposites, that there are healthy, active ways of living the cross as well. I would argue that the active mode of giving can also be a response to an invitation, not a demand, to live the cross and resurrection. As the refrain from an old Peter, Paul and Mary song put it:

In the instant of remaking
Just the giving of the taking
In the instant of the living
Just the taking of the giving.

We give to the world what we have "taken" from others and life, knowing that "taking" is a sacred receiving of the "giving" of others. This flowing dance between giving and taking can be a gracious, life long journey into wholeness.

To live into what we understand to be gospel values, to live into a self-emptying love, even at considerable cost to our social, economic and sometimes even our physical wellbeing can also offer us a profound way of living into the mystery of the cross and resurrection. Obviously, to be meaningful, any giving action on our part must flow from a free invitation, not a demand.

Some feel called to throw all caution to the wind, seeking justice and mercy in the world, and find this a liberating way to live. As Martin Luther King famously put it, "unmerited suffering is redemptive." I'm taking this to mean that any suffering freely taken upon ourselves to advance equality and mercy can be redemptive, both for those who choose it and for others who behold it. There is a powerful moral force available when we experience someone putting themselves on the line for a greater good, a higher truth, or when we make our own timid and tepid attempts to step into the consciousness of what Gandhi called "soul force."

To put it theologically, freely suffering for the sake of God's Kingdom (realm) bears fruit and gives life, perhaps the only life that is really worth living. I see Jesus, the Christ, as the bearer of this good news for humanity; by emptying himself of all self-strivings and filling himself with the revelation of God's present yet coming realm, by making God's dream of justice and equality his own, he may well have lived into a joy that transcends death and can never be extinguished.

As you eloquently put it, "He began to prophesy a huge change in history, the emergence of a world where the meek and the merciful, peacemakers and the persecuted, the humble and the hungry would become its citizens." While it isn't reported how this leveling of the playing field affected Jesus' spirit, we do know from many prophetic witnesses over time that there can be great meaning and purpose in living these values.

Thus, I believe that there is an active way of living the cross based on a willingness and even a gladness in taking on and bearing some of the "sins of the world" for the sake of God's realm. But as you imply, this needs to be guided by a genuine desire to serve and express love for humanity and not by an imperious inner demand for moral purity.

In a recent film, "The Law and the Prophets", Director Joshua Vis put it this way: Most prophets are "willing to risk something, to lose something, lose respect, lose influence, lose money, lose relationship, a life of choosing to lose. The life of most prophets is a life shaped by defeat. This is the secret of the prophets. They find meaning, even joy, in a worthy struggle, rooted in honesty, decency, integrity, courage and service. Victories are satisfying but they are fleeting. The worthy struggle is timeless."

Through the Cross and Resurrection, through this repeating cycle of in-breath and out-breath, Jesus invites us into both an active and a receptive way of joining with him, of participating with him in the "new order" that he proclaimed. If we seek to join Jesus the Christ in actively proclaiming God's coming realm, in witnessing to that land where the lion and lamb lie down together, a land where the rich and powerful no longer use the poor, then we'll probably have the opportunity to taste the bitter herbs of push-back, if not defeat. But those same herbs, through the miracle of "transubstantiation," can become sweeter than honey from living into that "new order." Perhaps entering into this cycle of dying and rising is one dimension of the glory that Irenaeus pointed to when he declared that "the glory of God is humanity fully alive."

However we choose to live the Cross and Resurrection, either through an ACTIVE GIVING out or an ACTIVE RECEIVING of God's compassion, or both, that will be our path into the divine flow of resting in, delighting in and becoming one with Presence. Through these modes of active participation in the Cross and Resurrection, we are gradually being re-imagined, re-formed and re-created into who we really are, the image of God.

RICHARD HIGGINS

In reading Carl Scovel's essay, I initially struggled with how to understand the crucifixion, which he describes with the precision of a Roman execution, as an act of compassion. Reading it takes me on my own harrowing journey into the hell of human suffering and cruelty. I am left at the foot of the cross, angry and bereft like one of the clueless, faithless disciples. How could this be an act of love? But yes, Good Friday is good, Scovel tell us, for it goes to the core of the Christian faith. It is a sign, he tells us, of God's redemptive love in an otherwise inexplicable suffering and death.

It is sign, too, of the crosses all of us must bear for the love of God. The essay tests my faith, but it also opens me to a deeper truth that cannot be explained. I rise from reading it invited into the mysterious truth that God's love for humanity shone that day on Golgotha.

JUDY HOEHLER

Kudos to Carl Scovel for this informative exploration of the history of the Cross in Christian theology. He sheds light on the rich tradition of Christ's descent into hell, a tradition little known in the Western mainline Protestantism in which I grew up. His explication of the Easter Icon in Orthodoxy was a revelation to me and deepened my understanding of the many-splendored Christianity of which I am a part.

I also appreciated his focus on historical misinformation in the New Testament, especially in the Fourth Gospel, that has led to anti-semitism among many Christians. So, too, with his observation that the church should not extol Constantine's pragmatic conversion to Christianity since this brought about the cross becoming a sign "not of God's compassion… [but] of the church's earthly power."

Carl seems to argue that the crucifixion is more significant than the resurrection in the biblical witness but I wonder if this is true. Metrics aside — how much space is devoted to descriptive details — I suggest that the crucifixion would have no significance without the resurrection. It was their resurrection experiences that convinced the early disciples Jesus was the Messiah. Without these experiences, no New Testament would have been written.

In addition to being a symbol of the crucifixion, the empty cross is also a symbol of the resurrection. In times of distress, it has been the Cross with its reminder that life is full of suffering but also of subsequent triumph that has sustained Christians down through the centuries.

But this is a minor criticism of what I consider a "must read" for those of us who grew up in that segment of Christianity that slips cheerfully from Palm Sunday to Easter morn without going through Good Friday.

SUSAN HOLMAN

Carl's essay asks one big question: How is it possible, given the world as we know it and Christianity's reputation for supporting violence, that we, who align with Jesus Christ and stand against such abuses, can call his cross and crucifixion anything "good"? It's a painful and honest question. I read his essay, for instance, on Christmas day, grieving unmitigated global human rights violations in the slaughter of women and children across the world. Doesn't thinking about the cross feed a mindset of violence?

Rather than respond directly to Carl's particular points, I will rather push at some of the nuances in his deeper concerns, through brief thoughts on some other texts that have shaped my thinking lately. One is patristic scholar Roberta Bondi's 'aha' moment on the meaning of the cross, told in her *Memories of God: Theological Reflections on a Life*.[1] One is a single line from Hildegard of Bingen's 12th century "Antiphon for the Crucified".[2] And one is Orkney writer, George Mackay Brown's poem, "The Harrowing of Hell." Each of these also reminds me of recent discussions with undergraduates about Matthias Grünewald's 'Isenheim Altarpiece,' an image Carl mentions in his essay.

First, in a true tale about a vivid moment in her "green-tiled bathroom," Roberta Bondi faced suddenly the disconnect between the early Christian

---

[1] Roberta C. Bondi, *Memories of God: Theological Reflections on a Life* (Nashville: Abingdon Press, 1995). My thoughts below are based on her Chapter 4, "Out of the Green-Tiled Bathroom: Crucifixion," pp. 111–144; the text quoted above is on p. 135.

[2] Hildegard of Bingen, "O cruor sanguinis: Antiphon for the Crucified," translated by Nathaniel M. Campbell, from the Riesenkodex, folio 466b, translation, music, and commentary posted on the International Society of Hildegard von Bingen Studies website, July 18, 2014. http://www.hildegard-society.org/2014/07/o-cruor-sanguinis-antiphon.html.

[3] George Mackay Brown, "The Harrowing of Hell," in Northern Lights (London: John Murray, 1999), 24. Preview with this poem is online at https://www. amazon.com/Northern-Lights-George-Mackay-Brown-ebook/dp/B00IA9RCOA/

writers she studied, and her personally more self-destructive 20th century Christian assumptions about the cross. Raised Baptist, seeped in the guilt of a childhood filled with Southern altar calls, she'd felt trapped into decades of depression and self-doubt with her family's toxic social idealization of women's self-sacrifice—fed explicitly by crucifixion ideals. It took her years of reading patristic authors, during doctoral studies at Oxford, authors who understood the cross more positively, before she 'got' it. In that green-tiled 'aha' moment, she saw that, as she put it,

> "In the equation 'sin + love + sacrifice = salvation' the early
> church redefined all the terms. They did not see sin as our
> hopeless badness….God did not love us sternly in spite of our
> unworthiness, nor was God or Jesus victimized by God's love….
> Jesus suffered not because suffering in itself is a necessary proof of
> love [but rather] in order that the hold death had on us would be
> loosened and the image of God be restored in us so that we could
> once again learn how to love."

Bondi does not deny the real damage done by the wrongs of an imperfect humanity in an imperfect world. But she does, like Carl, note with caution that how you interpret the crucifixion may depend on which Christian denominational hat you are wearing. For Bondi, those who make the Cross a front-and-center focus, and valorize Christ's gruesome pain and violent murder—miss the point. To model hope on a self-sacrificing bleeding god seems rather to make a sick joke if it fails to engage with the rest of the story. One gets stuck inside Grünewald's first, most gruesome and best-known panel: that of a diseased and purulent Christ in agony. Hope lies in the larger context, for instance the (equally weird but) exuberant resurrection scene and washes of light and air on the second panel.[4] And the healing potential of embodiedness in the sculptures and (yes, still pretty bizarre) painted saints of the third panel.

Grünewald's art, I remind my health science students, was meant to heal. The canvases, opened and shut in liturgical patterns, were housed in a monastic hospital alongside physicians, food and medicine, and therapeutic preaching. We may project troubling stereotypes on the green, wound-puckered running sores of the crucified body in the first panel if only because we, in our sanitized spaces, have (probably) never been that sick.

My students find more cheer in the Keiskamma altarpiece, a 20th century frame modeled deliberately on the Isenheim symbols but in different media: embroidered by a community of South African women in community devastated by the HIV/AIDS pandemic.[5] Yet both altarpieces point to healing. They do not praise pain or sacrifice. Both follow a long Christian tradition of cross as healer. "O stream of blood…anoint us and heal our feebleness," sang Hildegard of Bingen in her unfinished antiphon, 'O cruor sanguinis.' If life is in the blood, what anoints and helps must also be alive.

Holy Friday is "good," these suggest, not as a morbid memorializing that Jesus "died for our sins," but precisely because there was more to the story. The crucifixion breaks open spiritual capacity, with real-flesh implications to radically reify our very natural terror of mortality. Only by the crucifixion—*and what happened next*—can healing be more than a this-life Band-Aid, and enter instead into the paradoxical, mystical, corporal, and cosmic 'big bang' of what(ever) it was all about. Words fail, of course. I love Thomas Aquinas for having the good sense to shut up and put down his pen when, near the end of his life, he glimpsed this wonder. Perhaps our good sense is, with Hildegard, to sing.

---

[4] For the newly restored images, see now Joseph Nechvatal, "Restoration of the Isenheim Altarpiece," *Whitehot Magazine of Contemporary Art*, July 2022, https://whitehotmagazine.com/articles/restoration-isenheim-altarpiece/5460.

[5] For more on the Keiskamma embroidery, see e.g. Annette Wentworth, "Speaking in stitch: The *Keiskamma Altarpiece* as testimony to women's experience of the HIV/AIDS pandemic in South Africa," *Diaspora, Indigenous, and Minority Education* 15(4); 2021: 276–285. DOI: 10.1080/15595692.2021.1944088.

And then there's that Saturday. Carl points us to the traditions about the 'harrowing of hell.'[6] Art and poetry about Christ's routing out the underworld on Holy Saturday abound with long-fanged monsters, graveyards popping with surprised, half-dressed ex-corpses, and Jesus, perched over the abyss, legs apart like Superman, pulling with both arms as Adam and Eve shoot up from hellish mud.

Orkney writer, George Mackay Brown, a Catholic raised a Presbyterian, like Carl, has a wonderful poem about the harrowing of hell that is lovely for its understatements. Brown imagines Christ descending a circular seven-step stairway, going "down and round, clothed in his five wounds," to pull out the core of humankind's folly for all eternity. Halfway down he finds "At the root of the Tree…an urn / with dust of apple blossoms." And at the bottom, that familiar 'Ur-us': "the tall primal dust / Turned with a cry from digging and delving." What's it all for, we might ask? "Tomorrow," Brown breathes, "the Son of Man will walk in a garden / Through drifts of apple-blossom."

As Carl's essay reminds us, Christian clergy often spend their lives searching for the words that best 'get' these nuanced mysteries. The Orthodox Russian priest, Father Alexander Men, relating Christ's life in his *Son of Man*, could call it only the "paradox of the crucifixion and the mystery of the resurrection…the mystery with which his life was crowned."[7] Why is this crucifixion "good"? What is the meaning of hope, love, and justice? Perhaps it rests, in the end, on whatever is most true about that strange state of being we each, individually, and in community experience, treasure, and fear: that thing called life.

---

[6] On this tradition see Georgia Frank, "Christ's descent to the underworld in ancient ritual and legend," in *Apocalyptic Thought in Early Christianity*, ed. Robert J. Daly (Grand Rapids and Brookline, MA: Baker Academic and Holy Cross Orthodox Press, 2009), 211–226.

[7] Father Alexander Men, *Son of Man*, trans. Samuel Brown (Torrance, CA: Oakwood Press, 1998) pp. 4, 205.

CHRISTINE JARONSKI

The Museum of Russian Icons in Clinton, MA exhibits an icon that depicts a woman in Medieval dress with about a dozen knives in her chest. I am reminded of this in thinking about the crucifixion. Both the icon and the crucifixion present images that repel and compel. The icon drew me into a place of pain in my own heart – the anguish that I felt as my teenage son's brilliant mind was ravaged by schizophrenia. But it also led me to a sense that the spirit which inspired the icon understands my pain.

Similarly the crucifixion presents a repellent yet compelling image of compassion – love of the mother for her son, his love for her, and God's love for humanity. As it provokes our own compassion for Jesus' suffering, we also participate in God's love. We find a partner and a path through pain. We begin to understand the holiness of self sacrifice, and are able to see Christ "in the stranger's guise."

It has been 15 years since my son passed on through death; and the cross tells me that he is released into a new life – unknown to me, but still hoped for, for him, for me, for all of us.

LANE LAMBERT

If someone asked me to explain the Christian faith, I would give them Carl Scovel's essay. He has distilled a long ministerial career and a lifetime of reflection into a concise telling of Jesus' life, teaching, and sacrifice, and the story of the global faith he inspired. Carl bears necessary witness to the un-Christian violence and intolerance that are a dark part of Christianity's 2,000-year history, but he also draws the reader back to the love and actions that inspired Jesus' early followers — the life and love that continue to rescue the church from itself. In doing that, Carl doesn't just provide an introduction to Jesus for those who might not know anything about him. He also revives the inspiration and commitment of those of us who are trying faithfully to follow Jesus, here in the broken world of the 21st century. He has written a reflection for everyone.

BRIAN MASON

Three days after Christmas, I was carrying a casket across a graveyard. A man—a husband, father, son, and brother—had died.

A half-hour before the casket was lowered into the earth accompanied by Lynyrd Skynyrd's "Simple Man," the pastor officiating said something like this to the deceased's survivors: "God is with you. He's here now. He's right beside you. He's gone ahead. He's welcoming him home."

Some might shudder at such statements. "He can't know that!" we say. "How dare he?" we ask. Carl Scovel's answer might be as simple as *because he was one of us.* The "he" here refers to Jesus Christ. A man located in history as well as theology. A man who suffered and died. A man who felt betrayed by the very God of his being. A man whose friend carried his body to the grave. A man whose friends and family helplessly watched him die. The same friends and family who saw him — Magically? Mysteriously? Miraculously? — resurrected. And what did the resurrected Christ do? If we trust Luke's gospel, we know he talked with them and ate with them. After supper, he promised them the completion of the words of the prophets, the poetic justice of the psalms, and the Law of Moses. He blessed them with a vision of grace so grand it reached and still reaches into the grave.

Scovel's essay, first and foremost, is a pastoral tale. It tells of Christ's Crucifixion, what it means historically, religiously, and cosmically. It reads almost any way you want. As an introduction to some of Christianity's challenging bits. As a correction to abusive interpretations. But the essay is also a reminder of God's one-way love. Love that took on flesh. Love that saw humankind face to face, our best and worst, and loved us all the same.

It also conveys how strange and magical Communion is, which is a blessing. For in today's world, there seems a contagious zeal to dispense with tradition, especially religious ones.

Communion is something many of us have taken with great reverence— or pretended to. After all, that's what our Sunday school teachers taught us. But if we're honest, we've taken it half-awake too. But Communion, channeling Annie Dillard, is best done wearing a crash helmet. It requires extra protection because getting our guard up helps us remember that when we approach the altar, we're not alone. The saints are there, both living and dead. I imagine death row inmates there as well, ICU patients, white-robed kids from first Communions past. It's an act as marvelous as the universe rendered simply into bread and wine. It is, in Scovel's words, a meal taken in the name of a man whose inhabiting of human form left us with a "love which this world lacks." I think of Communion as that time in a church service when friends alongside strangers accept God's dare to believe what He said with our entire being: that God loved the whole world. All of it.

How we arrive as this enveloping love is shocking. Jesus' story takes us from the womb to the tomb in terrifying fashion. A common question in response to Jesus' life is "Why?" Some of Christianity's "why's" are answerable, but not all. Maybe not even most. However, one of the why's we're given is this: God loves. God loves us when we're sick and tired, addicted or sober, living, dying or dead. On your wedding day, or when your kid runs a 104-degree fever, or when you are confined in an internment camp, or when you are being lowered into the ground, God is there.

One remarkable thing about the funeral in which I held the man's casket came, for me, when his youngest daughter, well into adulthood, eulogized her father. She told it all. She gave us a portrait in such vivid detail that you felt as though you'd been given a secret spot on the wall to watch his life. The sordid bits, which neither the preacher nor the daughter ignored, did nothing to stop the congregation's eyes from misting over with a love not only for the family amid their grief, but for the man. A man whose story reminded us that love has the power to break into the toughest places. Love like this comes from only one place: grace.

God's grace is the great disrupter. It disrupts our assumptions. It disrupts generational trauma. It inspires justice, it lessens dogma, it invites questions. It is, to use Scovel's words, moments "When we act out of our own being loved." Or, to remix Scovel's phrase, grace is when love acts on us. When gratitude and love find us as we carry a casket across the frozen ground. When we relax into the care of someone who has dedicated themselves to our care, to the care of the sick, the care of the scared. Or when we're humbled by the depth of someone's sacrifice. But especially when we ourselves break bread and dare to believe that God is here. Now. Beside us. Ahead of us. Calling us home.

DAVE O'NEAL

Thanks for sending your thoughtful and mind-expanding piece. **I am probably too much a heretic to respond to it properly.**

Yeah, when I say that, to me, the cross and resurrection are the same thing, I mean it deeply. The fact that no other founder of religion died like Christ is irrelevant to me. They WOULD have died as he did, I think, because they set themselves in the direction of compassion, which they learned, was the only honest thing one can do, when one sees the reality of one's fellow human.

I've always had a problem with Christ's death as atonement. Atonement for what? Compassion is the important thing, and it is not separate from intelligence. In the Mediterranean world they were already learning creative ways to make fun of the less fortunate; to blame the poor for their own poverty; to find new ways to be sexual, using other people for that ostensibly. Christianity was a radical response to that. But so were the many people who woke up, and who (always inadvertently) became the founders of a religion.

It's just that their own practice sets them in the direction of compassion. It's the only reasonable response!

Like I said, I've always had a problem with atonement, and our Orthodox Church, as wonderful as it is with it's true apophasis, tends to mitigate Christ's death, or to make it (along with the evangelical heretics who are storming in) just go away. This is kinda why I hate Pascha but love Lent. In Pascha we tend to hope that Christ's death didn't really happen.

And the fact that Gospel accounts don't match up (especially John) they don't consider. To me that not-matching is very important. It shows that this resurrection should disappear before us and be very hard. But they get very defensive about it.

So maybe you'll see why I say Cross and Resurrection are the same thing. Resurrection is inherent (I think) in every act of compassion no matter how big or small. It all goes against the grain of the way things usually are.

KATHERINE HALL PAGE

I am looking at my Unitarian Sunday School enameled attendance pin— bars attached marking eleven years. It has a cross in red bisecting a shiny gold crown indicating life in heaven hereafter. Our Montclair, New Jersey church had a large cross on the altar. The cross as a symbol of Christ's Crucifixion and the mystery of the Resurrection have been constant companions on my lifelong journey in faith.

Some thoughts spurred by Carl Scovel's "How The Cross Came Out Of The Crucifixion." It has been a provocative pleasure to read the essay.

In December 2023 I saw art at the Prado in Spain that I had only seen in reproductions and the experience was an intensely spiritual one as I moved through the museum all day. I found myself stopping longest not at the famous portraits and still lifes, but the religious works—Christ on the cross, the Deposition—many works by artists unknown to me, arresting images.

The crucifixion was horrific as was the torture and humiliation that preceded it. The blood of Christ is our blood, it glistens on the canvas. His corpse, in contrast to those surrounding him, is not pale, but blue tinged, "livor mortis" as ours will be. Many of the paintings are huge, altar pieces that depict a story for a populace that could not read. There is no mistaking the message. Carl Scovel says it well, "Jesus, God's own Son, was one of us, as mortal in death as in life."

We are meant to look at him and be him. His suffering is *our* suffering.

And then comes the Resurrection. I have struggled with this, and still do. It requires a kind of suspension of belief in the natural word; in science. As a devout Unitarian I assumed I would go back into the earth and rise as a birch or oak, but this belief has never satisfied me, sensible as it may be. When Carl asked me to react to this essay, I recalled a paper I wrote in 1966 for a (then) required year-long course in the Bible at Wellesley College. I found the draft among some old papers. The assignment was to imagine Christ's last three days! I had not read it since and was slightly astounded to find a description echoing some of what Carl Scovel is saying.

I wrote that "Peter saw an urgency he had never seen in his master before. More often now Jesus became angered at the perversity of man's unbelief... They entered Jerusalem and Peter saw that there were more enemies than believers and he became afraid. Jesus seemed to be drawing more apart from them in an energy which was beyond comprehension." I wrote about Christ's fear of his own death and described him walking off, "looking not at the horizon, but at the stones and dust beneath his feet." He has asked his disciples to stay awake, but returning finds them, even Peter, asleep and knows that he will die. Jesus is walking to death, to the crucifixion and thus frees us from our fear of it, affirming our place in life—our membership, bestowed at birth. Scovel expresses this beautifully as walking "toward death, *into* death and *through* death to live that love which death could not, cannot and can *never conquer.*"

As for the Resurrection, in another passage in the paper I wrote many years ago, these words as if from Christ: "I have partaken of death since I last saw you and have risen to tell you, my disciples, of this communion… I have risen to give man the gift of faith I failed to give them before. I have now seen that which all men before me have seen and all men after me shall see. I have risen to bring man a torch out of the limitless darkness he fears, so he may know that the Kingdom of God is a Kingdom of light."

This is the gift, the good news that I take from this essay. That "We can only give what we've been given," to quote from it further, "God loved us first." That God is the kind of God William Sloane Coffin described after his own son's death, "God's heart was the first of all our hearts to break." When we take communion, we join the living and the risen Christ. Thanks be to God.

The last day of our trip to Spain was December 8th, the Feast of the Immaculate Conception. We entered the Iglesia de San Matias, which we later learned was the parish church of Saint Matthew erected inside a mosque in 1501. The two existed together until Charles V had razed the building, erecting a Baroque church on the long, narrow space.

The church was full when we entered and the congregation was saying the Hail Mary. It sounded very musical in Spanish. We watched as people quietly took their places in line to venerate with a kiss the almost life-sized statue of the virgin placed below the altar. The act felt like thanks, it felt like love and thinking now, an "enactment." In my mind I hear Julian's, and God's promise, "All shall be well, and all shall be well, and all manner of things shall be well."

JOHN PASTOR

In my nearly twenty years of hospice ministry, I have witnessed the symbols of the crucifixion and the cross used by my patients in their own spiritually comforting ways and in their own understanding of the process of death and dying. I've come to learn that for these patients the crucifix is a symbol of suffering and the cross is a symbol of hope.

In some Christian churches the crucifix, with Jesus on the cross, is the primary symbol of His suffering and it is venerated. For these churches it is central to their belief that Jesus' suffering was necessary for the world's redemption. The crucifix, therefore, for these folks is a profound and sacred symbol of suffering.

Over the years I have witnessed this belief in my patients; that dying is rightly surrounded by suffering, by pain. This was often true for devout patients who would refuse medication for pain because, as they told me, they needed to feel the pain to know that they were alive. They also shared that they had to suffer through death for Jesus' sake as they were focused on the crucifix.

In other Christian churches there is no crucifix displayed, just the cross, sine corpus. Jesus is blessedly absent from the cross. It can be very comforting that Jesus is not hanging and suffering on the cross. It does much to foster the belief that He indeed is risen. This encourages Christians to live in "certain hope of the Resurrection." For these of Jesus' faithful, the empty cross is a symbol of hope.

The crucifix as suffering. The cross as hope.

Hope is the reason that Christianity has survived despite all the many centuries of non-Christian behaviors that the world has endured in Jesus' name.

I had not seen Carl in person for some time. After COVID was contained, we had a lengthy catch-up lunch. During our valued time together, Carl shared his experience of having prostate cancer. He told of the months of drugs and treatments with the side effects of nausea, fatigue, and diarrhea. At the end of his sharing Carl said, "I wouldn't have missed it for the world." Knowing Carl, I was not too surprised by this. For I believed then and I believe now, that he, like some of my patients, may have needed to feel pain to know that he was alive. I further believe that this has changed him, hence his reflective essay. He has moved through his suffering to a new, or perhaps transformed hope, and a reformed way of knowing that he is still alive. Carl has moved from a perceived crucifix to the cross and now perhaps more fervently believes, as Julian of Norwich proclaims, "You will never be overcome."

In his essay Carl refers to Christian worship focused on Good Friday, Holy Saturday, and Easter Sunday. Holy Thursday, the Last Supper, of course, is also an important inclusion in these Jesus events. All these sacred days have become a major formation focus of the Christian faith.

But I propose that a later Jesus event, the Ascension, is included as formation foundation. The Ascension holds an important message of hope that is essential to understanding the Christian faith. Christians are called to live with hope. Can there be faith if there is no hope?

Before His Ascension into heaven, it is reported that Jesus told His followers that He would come back. This leaves the comforting notion of Jesus returning. But they didn't know when He would return. He did not say when. Later disciples, saints and prophets, especially Paul, urged people to remain faithful and to be patient, waiting for Jesus the Savior to return. Decades and centuries have passed and the faithful and questioning faithful still wait. Christianity has survived by hope.

Today's Christians are modern-day followers with eyes up to heaven and looking around the earth, like our ancestors of old, for certainty in an uncertain world. They are on an unpredictable journey together seeking Jesus. In this regard the cross continues to beacon the hope for the return of Jesus the Christ.

Christ has died. Christ is risen. Christ is ascended. Christ will come again.

TERRY VAUGHN

In the following section the words of the text appear in Roman type, *the response in italics.*

And who did go ? The women: first, the four Mary's – Mary his mother, Mary of Magdala, Mary the wife of Clopas, Mary the mother of James and Joses;. then the mother of the Zebedee brothers, a woman named Salome, and the women from Galilee. "Last at the cross and first at the tomb," women witnessed his death and announced his resurrection.

It is noteworthy that "the disciple whom Jesus loved" is also at the cross (and later outruns Peter to the tomb.) Tradition holds that this disciple is the writer of John's gospel. On the cross Jesus utters an important exclamation directed both at this disciple and his own mother, "Son, behold your mother" and "Mother, behold your son." (John 19:26)

"The aim of Holy Communion is to feed the soul through feeding the body. This mini-meal reverberates with memories of meals with family, friends and congregations in the past. It reverberates with the knowledge that on the Lord's Day (the first name for Sunday) Christians around the world are receiving Christ's presence in churches, chapels, cathedrals or their homes."

As bread and wine Holy Communion nourishes the body. That is precisely its sacramental value in being the real body and blood, the soul and divinity, of Jesus. It effects what it symbolizes, nourishment for the body and soul par excellence! The revulsion that some feel concerning the Orthodox and Catholic understanding of the Eucharist echoes the revulsion that many of Jesus' disciple felt (John 6: 60–62). When Jesus in response says "Would you also turn away?", Peter replies, "Where have we to go but you? You have the words of eternal life." (John 6:68)

"Twenty years after the crucifixion Christians were celebrating communion. We find the seed of Holy Communion in Paul's first letter to the Christian church in Corinth. This "seed" begins with a rebuke, for it seems that the Christians in Corinth had turned the Lord's Supper in a chaotic free-for all."

I find it significant that in the liturgy of St. John Chrysostom the Eucharistic words spoken over the bread (called the Lamb) are "This is my body which broken for you" and those spoken over the cup are "the Blood which is poured out for you." In the Latin rite, the Mass, the large host (the bread) is dramatically broken while the choir intones the Agnus Dei, "Lamb of God, who takes away the sins of the world." "Worthy is the Lamb who was slain" writes the book of Revelation (5:12).

For Catholic and Orthodox the Eucharistic Liturgy is not a re-enactment of the Last Supper. It is a reenactment of the sacrificial death on the cross in which Christ breaks Himself, yes, recreates His death on the cross. The Last Supper is a pre-enactment of the sacrificial death at Golgotha, all of this prefigured in the institution of the Passover as described in Exodus 12.

It is also noteworthy that Christ's death occurred precisely when the Paschal lambs were being slain in the Temple. The Eucharistic Liturgy, which is Holy Communion, is a meal, but a sacrificial meal enacted by Christ through the ministry of the presiding bishop or priest with the great affirmation of the people's "Amen."

"That is why Paul writes, "For as often as you eat this bread and drink this cup, you proclaim the Lord's death until he comes." Why does Paul say that the liturgy proclaims the Lord's death and not His life. We can only conclude that the Lord's death is a life-giving death, the death which gave birth to the church and new life to each Christian. We see this again in Romans 6:3 where Paul reminds Christians that they were baptized into his death."

The Mass of the Latin rite says this explicitly when the presiding priest proclaims, "Let us proclaim the Mystery of Faith," and the people respond, "Christ has died. Christ has Risen. Christ shall come again."

In the Byzantine Liturgy of the Orthodox and Greek Catholic churches the priest recites that beautiful prayer which commemorates Christ's command, the cross, the tomb, the resurrection, the ascension and Christ's return.

"The church asserts that the risen Jesus is present at Holy Communion. Different households of faith differ on how Christ is present, but affirm that Christ is present."

Yes, it is ultimately the mystery of faith. The Catholic church's insistence on the term "transubstantiation" is not an explanation of the mystery, but an affirmation that the mystery is real in the most graphic sense of what is REAL. It is what the words say it is. The bread and wine's substance (reality) has been transformed while all the accidents (color, taste, texture) remain to feed us as Christ Himself is feeding us with this real, resurrected Bodily Presence.

THOMAS D. WINTLE

When I was young someone told me that the difference between a crucifix (with the body of Jesus on the cross) and a plain cross was the difference between Roman Catholics and Protestants — that the Catholics focused on the crucifixion as the redeeming event and Protestants focused on the resurrection, thus the empty cross. That is an oversimplification, to be sure, but questions abound. Was the cross a sign of failure, the worst that humanity can do to a person, the expression of the suffering that lies at the heart of the human condition, to be redeemed only by the resurrection? That seems to be the way most liberals view the crucifixion.

Or was the cross more? Did it somehow change the relationship of God and humanity? What a far cry from that cross of suffering are the liturgical words "We adore thee, O Christ, and we praise thee because by thy cross and passion thou hast redeemed the world" and "Through his cross the Lord Jesus brought salvation to the human race" (Roman Catholic).

Carl does not use the word "atonement" – certainly not in the sense of the death of Christ somehow satisfying God's honor in the face of humanity's disobedience. But the idea that the crucifixion brings God and humanity back together, reconciles and makes us new, does bring at-one-ment.

Anglican Geoffrey Tristram writes of "the profound mystery at the heart of the Christian faith. That we can come to the foot of the cross and bring our hurts and failures, even our greatest pain, and know what it is to be held in God's love. And then most mysteriously of all, to experience that pain mysteriously transformed, transfigured, by the love of God, and to be taken up into the resurrection of Christ" (SSJE, Cambridge).

Which is the saving event – death or resurrection? And which moves the heart? I think the liturgy has it right: Both. Good Friday (and silent Saturday) and Easter are one event, not to be separated, the Triduum.

Carl Scovel calls liberals to resurrect the deeper meaning of the cross, to take its role in salvation more seriously. The crucifixion is not just sad, it frees us. It is Good Friday.

Per crucem et passionem tuam
Libera nos domine,
Libera nos domine,
Libera nos domine,
Domine.

THE RESPONDENTS

KATE BAKER-CARR, an ordained UCC pastor, has served students as a college chaplain and congregations as a parish minister. For many years she worked as a business planning and communications executive, first in health care and then in higher education. Now retired from full-time employment, she continues to mentor candidates for ministry and provides coverage for clergy on vacation or sabbaticals. She preaches regularly and is an active member of her home church in Brookline, MA.

ANITA FARBER-ROBERTSON, has ministerial standing in the Unitarian Universalist Association and among the American Baptist Churches. She was the settled minister at The First Parish in Canton, MA and served ten other churches as an interim minister. Active in local and national elections and in the civil rights and peace movements, she has volunteered in service projects and organizations in Swampscott, MA, where she has lived for over forty years. She has raised four offspring and in her younger days hiked in the White Mountains. She worships at Zion Baptist Church in Lynn, MA.

MY UNNAMED FRIEND writes "My life's journey has had many unpredictable twists and turns, including training as a paramedic, a doctorate degree, life as a university professor, and decades of work in social justice here and abroad, particularly in the support, mentoring, protection and education of children. I think of myself as a dedicated life-long learner. In both my intellectual and theological life I am constantly asking questions and searching for patterns, trying to find ways for things to make sense. Carl has been one of the most important guides who has walked beside me on this journey and for whom I am immeasurably grateful."

STEPHEN FISHER is a spiritually oriented psychologist in private practice who feels at home and is enlivened by breathing the fresh, open theological air of a Unitarian Christian church, King's Chapel in Boston. He is happily married to Cynde Reilly and lives in Westford, MA. Steve feels humbled "before the abundance always pouring forth and graciously given. Ever so silently and seamlessly, the Gracious One has drawn and accompanied me out of spiritual poverty." He finds that laughter is the best medicine!

RICHARD HIGGINS is a writer and editor in Concord, Massachusetts, and the author of *Thoreau and the Language of Trees*. His new book, *Thoreau's God*, will be published in the fall of 2024.

JUDY HOEHLER, Minister Emerita of the First Parish Church in Weston, MA, now lives in Seattle, WA, with her husband of 68 years. Active in her neighborhood UCC church, she volunteers at a local library and enjoys daily walks, reading, live concerts and conversation with friends & family over dinner.

SUSAN HOLMAN is the John R. Eckrich Chair and Professor of Religion and the Healing Arts at Valparaiso University. A writer by vocation, she grew up in the Lutheran Church-Missouri Synod. A Tertiary of the Order of the Holy Paraclete, a monastic community based in the UK, she currently worships alongside the global communion of Orthodox Christians.

CHRISTINE JARONSKI served as pastor of the First Church (UCC) in Charlestown, MA from 2000 to 2008. A graduate of Barnard College and the Harvard Divinity School, she was ordained by King's Chapel in 1996. A love of music, especially singing, has been a life-long blessing. She has taught piano and sung with several choral groups, including the Tanglewood Festival Chorus for ten years. Married, she is the mother of two sons and grandmother of three boisterous boys in Germany.

LANE LAMBERT, a writer and journalist, is a United Methodist layman in Boston, MA.

BRIAN MASON is a Christian pastor ordained to the Unitarian Universalist ministry, serving a congregation in the Midwest.

DAVE O'NEAL grew up in an old California family in that state's central valley. He served in the US Coast Guard from 1972–1976, mostly in Alaska, and lived on Kodiak Island until 1984. He converted to Eastern Orthodoxy in 1979 and graduated from Humboldt State University and St. Vladimir's Seminary. He had a long career in publishing, mostly as Senior Editor at Shambhala Publications. He has practiced Zen Buddhism from 1988 to the present. For thirty years he practiced Orthodox Christianity. His essays and poetry can be read on his blog, Non-Idiomatic(davensati54.blogspot.com).

KATHERINE HALL PAGE identifies as a Christian Unitarian and is a longtime member of King's Chapel in Boston and a Friend of St. Anne's in-the-Fields Episcopal church, Lincoln, MA. After a career as a high school teacher and administrator, she turned to full-time writing. Over thirty of her books have been published, most of them in the Faith Fairchild Mystery series. She writes "The traditional mystery is characterized by endings in which justice prevails, order triumphs and the universe is a benign one." In so doing she has felt blessed in both jobs to unite her vocation with her avocation, echoing Robert Frost's "As my two eyes make one in sight."

JOHN PASTOR, an ordained Unitarian Universalist minister, has served congregations in parish churches and hospice patients and their loved ones as their spiritual caregiver. Now retired he volunteers as a Patient Liaison at a local hospital. He is honored to have Carl as a friend, colleague and mentor.

TERRY VAUGHN was born and baptized into a staunch Roman Catholic family. He says, "I pursued my faith as a young man with gusto, only to fall into the grip and lure of 'demi-monde' later in life. I rediscovered my faith and its riches in a small, rural Russian Orthodox church where I met my dear wife. Disillusioned by some of that church's intransigent positions regarding ecumenism, we found common spiritual roots in the Ukrainian Greek Catholic Church. Earlier in my life I was fortunate to find inspiration and deepen my understanding of the faith from some erudite theological professors at the Catholic University of America, MA."

TOM WINTLE has retired after twenty years as pastor of the First Church of Christ Unitarian (gathered in 1653) in Lancaster, MA, and twenty-three years as senior minister of the First Parish Church (gathered in 1698) in Weston, MA. Like T. S. Eliot and others, Tom journeyed from Unitarianism to high church Anglo-Catholicism. He has been a member of the Fellowship of the Society of St. John the Evangelist since 1993. For thirty years he was the editor of a theological journal, *The Unitarian Universalist Christian*.

Twenty-three hundred feet over the city of Rio de Janeiro stands this nine-hundred foot statue of Jesus. His posture reminds us that on the cross he also held out his arms as if to say, "Come to me all you who labor and bear heavy burdens, I will give you rest."

I was eleven years old when I saw this statue for the first time as I stood at the stern of a ship taking me, our family and twelve hundred other Americans from internment camps in Asia to New York City. There we saw in the harbor another statue which promised us safety and freedom.

ACKNOWLEDGMENTS

I want to thank the fifteen friends who read my essay, and took the time and effort to write their responses. This text is the richer for their contributions.

I could not have written this essay without the faith and wisdom I've received through the priests and people of Holy Trinity Orthodox Cathedral in Boston. Nor could I be who I am without my two Jesuit spiritual directors, Bill Barry and Paul Lucey, companions on my journey toward God. The friendship and challenges of my Unitarian Universalist colleagues has forced me continually to ask myself, "What do I believe? What and Whom do I trust?"

I want to thank Tom Wintle who gave time and care to editing this text and counseling me in its evolution. Our fifty years of friendship have been a gift. It was through Tom's initiative that the Evangelical Missionary Society decided to support the publication of this book.

The cover and pages of this book were designed by Victoria Sax. She is a joy to work with and her competence is evident on these pages and earlier in my collection of marriage quotes titled *I DO*.

Faith, my wife of sixty-six years, has not only read and edited my essay, she has also endured without reproach my many hours of absence during this project, accepting my strange obsession with religion and writing.

Finally, I thank you, my readers. You are the completion of our labors.

Carl Scovel